© **Life Quotes For One and All**
BY SANDEEP RAVIDUTT SHARMA

Table of Contents

Foreword IV

Life Quotes For One and All 1

© **Life Quotes For One and All**
BY SANDEEP RAVIDUTT SHARMA

Foreword

This book provides you with a list of **100** quotes and thoughts about LIFE, churned out by my mind with the consciousness, grace and energy of **Shiva Shakti**.

I'm sure if you keep reading, referring and sharing these thoughts and quotes about LIFE, you may derive inspiration and develop good understanding of various perspectives and facts. These quotes can reiterate your commitment towards living a responsible and cheerful life. It would help you to focus on your present and LIVE NOW instead of going back in the past or thinking too much about the future.

"Life pages keep turning on its own and presents both surprise and shock. Grab your share and LIVE NOW"

I sincerely hope, you will find this book amazing, interesting, rejuvenating, unique and a constant source of Inspiration.

Thank You and Happy Reading.

© **Life Quotes For One and All**
BY SANDEEP RAVIDUTT SHARMA

Copyright © 2018
by Sandeep Ravidutt Sharma

All rights reserved. No part of this book may be reproduced or transmitted in any form or by any means without written permission from the author.

If you have further questions, contact on

Phone: +919969256731
Email: sandeepraviduttsharma@gmail.com

© **Life Quotes For One and All**
BY SANDEEP RAVIDUTT SHARMA

Dedication

This book is dedicated to **Shiva Shakti** - the epitome of love. Lord Shiva is pure consciousness symbolising the masculine principle. Goddess Shakti symbolises the active feminine energy of Shiva and is synonymously identified with **Tripura Sundari, Sati** or **Parvati**. These primal principles are also called as PURUSHA representing consciousness and PRAKRITI denoting the nature. Shiva and Shakti are manifestations of the all-in-one divine consciousness. Shiva is the paternal love of God that gives us consciousness, knowledge and clarity. Shakti is the motherly love of God that showers warmth, care and ensures our protection. Shiva and Shakti exist within each of us as the masculine and feminine energy.

To please **Shiva Shakti** praying for the well being, love, happiness, strength, positive energy and success of my readers in their life, i hereby recite the following mantra...

"Sarva Mangala Mangalye Shive Sarvartha Sadhike Sharanye Tryambake Gauri Narayani Namostute"

© **Life Quotes For One and All**
BY SANDEEP RAVIDUTT SHARMA

Photo Credits

The amazing and soothing photograph used in this book as a Cover and backdrop for the inside pages are clicked by **Anna Maritta** from **Germany**. You can visit her excellent photo gallery at

Instagram: @Anna_Maritta_0107

© **Life Quotes For One and All**
BY SANDEEP RAVIDUTT SHARMA

Life Quotes For One and All

© **Life Quotes For One and All**
BY SANDEEP RAVIDUTT SHARMA

Rare Gems are those who empty their pockets for others and still smile.

© **Life Quotes For One and All**
BY SANDEEP RAVIDUTT SHARMA

Today get inspiration from the Sun. Sun follows discipline, believes in giving without expecting anything in return, faces its own heat for the world but never complains. Sun thwarts dark forces not just for a day but the battle is on for billions of years. Be a Sun for the world.

© **Life Quotes For One and All**
BY SANDEEP RAVIDUTT SHARMA

Great men never say or pretend to be Great.

It's the duty of each generation to pass on the knowledge gained to the next generation and also warn them of certain misuse.

© **Life Quotes For One and All**
BY SANDEEP RAVIDUTT SHARMA

Don't misuse the word 'Sorry' every now and then. Be more responsible of your actions and make attempt to correct in time.

© **Life Quotes For One and All**
BY SANDEEP RAVIDUTT SHARMA

Watch the world not just by your eyes but through your heart. LIFE is beautiful.

Nature ensures harmony.

People declare whether your attitude is bad or good. You always have the option to change it.

Your eyes capture LIFE moments, memory records it, heart desires to recall and mind helps to retrieve them. Sometimes the recalled moments lead to tears of joy or sadness.

Accidental win doesn't last long. Be consistent and improve everyday for a sustainable win.

No one likes a critic who always meet you with a mirror. Take Critics as your real friends. They don't allow you to remain with a flaw and are likely to tell the whole world. All you have to do is pay heed to their criticism and do course correction. Thank to all the critics who put you on the path of perfection.

When you look around with a refreshing mind, everyone or everything would seem to inspire. Let this inspiration flow to whosoever you meet.

LIFE is a journey. You can take a break for sometime but then you have to resume with full force and march ahead on your LIFE path. So my dear friend, Keep Going...

© **Life Quotes For One and All**
BY SANDEEP RAVIDUTT SHARMA

Don't bother about the world. Live your LIFE the way you like, but with responsibility and ease.

Begin your day with the following thought..... Today is my day. I'm here to achieve what I have thought of. To win I will leave no stone unturned. Sincerity and consistency of efforts will be my hall mark.

Achievement doesn't come overnight. It's a result of dedicated efforts with a self belief.

Don't bother about what someone would steal from you, focus more on what more you can give and share.

© **Life Quotes For One and All**
BY SANDEEP RAVIDUTT SHARMA

Great men don't complain but ensures nobody complains in future.

Next step is known only when the first one is in place

© **Life Quotes For One and All**
BY SANDEEP RAVIDUTT SHARMA

LIFE lessons never gets over. At every step you have got something to learn. There is no age limit for learning. Don't shy away from learning.

Never share secrets unless it benefits humanity.

© Life Quotes For One and All
BY SANDEEP RAVIDUTT SHARMA

Raise your hand to express your intent when opportunity calls.

Express your joy even if others don't understand the same.

Explore the world and you will be amazed.

It's raining happiness if you can see.

Power of people throws incompetent ones sooner or later.

Just posing with the Divine Sun makes you glow. Keep up with the right company and you can never go wrong.

Why get influenced by others when you have decided to become an influencer.

Don't miss out to thank everyone who could help you in some way or the other.

Complex situations can have simple solutions. LIFE appears to be complex but it is simple to live provided you leave aside baggage of past and ghosts of the future. Focus only on today...and NOW to be more specific.

© **Life Quotes For One and All**
BY SANDEEP RAVIDUTT SHARMA

Don't play hide n seek with LIFE. You can't hide from LIFE challenges without seeking timely solution.

© **Life Quotes For One and All**
BY SANDEEP RAVIDUTT SHARMA

Try your best to stay positive even when tides are not in your favour.

© **Life Quotes For One and All**
BY SANDEEP RAVIDUTT SHARMA

Don't postpone your celebration for the day.

When you reach stage of excellence the level of expectations will rise manifold. Let these expectations motivate you to reach greater heights.

When anger rules your mind and venomous words are spoken. You may still believe that you are correct. Later on you may realise and feel that it could have been handled differently. Hold your words when anger rules.

Visualize the World as cheer leaders who are celebrating your win whenever they laugh at you.

Look for peace if crowd makes you angry.

Poverty and misery are the real test posed by the Lord for the rich to see whether they do enough to wipe this out and bring smile on the face of the poor.

Don't fear anyone when you talk. The commonality between all of us is that we are first human than Sweeper or the King.

Don't practice discrimination of any kind.

Don't expect well laid path for your smooth journey. Many of us have to lay the path before we can even walk.

Sometimes what's right in front of you fades and the background becomes prominent. Nothing has changed it's just change of your attention and focus.

People may forget your failure but you need to remember it till you try again and win.

Today if you had an appointment with Failure, don't get discouraged. Lessons learnt today along with your strong resolve to try again can attract Success soon.

Raise your voice if your legitimate demands are not heard.

When you practice kindness you not only get blessings from the people of our world but even from the divine forces.

Act in time and and not just discuss. Success befriends your act and not necessarily your words.

You don't really own anything in this world except your deeds. Even dedicate or renounce these deeds in the name of the Lord.

Escape from the past by living in the present.

Your anger can become your weapon if you need to attack the tyrant and save innocent lives.

Evaluate a proposal with open mind without getting influenced by anyone or anything. Timely evaluation can save the execution time.

No plane can fly you to your destination unless you have decided to board.

Thank everyone and everything in this world who is concerned and share their time, wealth, wishes and positive vibes. Without their support LIFE would be meaningless and ordinary.

Don't expect to shine all the time, even Sun retires in the evening and gives Moon and Stars a chance to shine and drive away darkness.

If you have mastered Law of Attraction and has attracted or accumulated tons of money but not using it on your own self or for helping others. Such wealth is like rusted iron which appears to be strong from outside but gets deteriorated from inside.

When few exceptions are introduced, rule becomes weak. When exceptions outnumber the compliance, rule is dead.

Don't over think or else the world will slip away from you.

People may come and walk out of your LIFE. You can't control their behavior and avoid getting drowned in their memories. Value those who are with you and don't cry for those who have deserted you. Be who you are and not don the image of a lost soul.

Inspire others with your deeds and thoughts.

© **Life Quotes For One and All**
BY SANDEEP RAVIDUTT SHARMA

Fill your mind with positive thoughts and attract the best in your LIFE.

Inspiration is all around us. Even if darkness surrounds you and instills fear in you. Look at the Moon and Stars for inspiration.

When you meet strangers in LIFE. They may become your friends or foe depending on whether you use Treat or Threat approach.

There is no shortcut to getting rich except dedicated efforts based on a well thought out plan.

When you move in the right direction SUCCESS will be all yours.

There is no shortcut to success in LIFE. Consistent efforts mixed with determination and a great attitude can put you on the road to success.

Nothing is better than freedom.

Sometimes what you see may not be the truth that doesn't mean what you hear was the truth.

© **Life Quotes For One and All**
BY SANDEEP RAVIDUTT SHARMA

Fill the mind with positive affirmation and see the difference.

© **Life Quotes For One and All**
BY SANDEEP RAVIDUTT SHARMA

Waves come and go, few of them are motivated enough to touch the shore, some of them return half way. Same way people come in and go from our LIFE, few of them are good enough to touch our heart and remembered.

Don't play hide and seek with your LIFE. Don't hide when you are called to perform and win. Don't seek happiness when you hardly worked for it.

When anger takes over even a thought leader becomes its slave.

LIFE makes you rich or poor depending on how you want to treat your own self.

Don't just come to conclusions about anyone without making attempt to understand the facts available. We generally rush to conclusion and regret later.

Keep Going. Things which stops moving becomes history.

Today is your day.

Practice Forgiveness. Forgiveness helps you to stay calm and gives second chance to the other person for initiating course correction. When you practice the virtue of forgiveness, your soul is purified and you enjoy bliss of God.

© **Life Quotes For One and All**
BY SANDEEP RAVIDUTT SHARMA

Why do millions of people worldwide say 'Good Morning' in their respective language? The answer is simple, by default we are more inclined towards negative emotions. Positivity needs to be reinforced by us on a regular basis. We have to keep reminding ourselves and others that it's a great day to start with. Positive affirmation wipes out negativity and helps us to win.

© **Life Quotes For One and All**
BY SANDEEP RAVIDUTT SHARMA

Greatness is not achieved in a day. It requires constant efforts dipped in knowledge sauce and frequent churning. Most of the time the doer doesn't know that he is on the path to achieve greatness.

Keep faith in the Lord and fear is no more.

© **Life Quotes For One and All**
BY SANDEEP RAVIDUTT SHARMA

LIFE pages keep turning automatically even if you are passive.

Sometimes when the world laughs at you don't show your irritation and help them to rejoice more. Practice silence, work on perfecting your skills, wait for the opportunity, perform and have the last laugh.

With purity of thoughts and good deeds, you can feel the presence of the God in everything around you and right within your heart.

Never take appointment for disappointment of any kind.

© **Life Quotes For One and All**
BY SANDEEP RAVIDUTT SHARMA

Explore your own self and you will be enlightened.

Waves are under the false impression that together they can sink the Sun. Next morning the winning spell is broken when Sun shines again in the Sky and Waves just look and in frustration move to and fro the shore throughout the day.

There is slight difference between Word and World. Word can make your world if it is painted with Likeness Love or Laughter

© **Life Quotes For One and All**
BY SANDEEP RAVIDUTT SHARMA

When you meet someone it's not just a one off meeting without a purpose. The agenda of your chance meeting is fixed by the Lord and there is a reason behind it. So have faith in God who has written the entire script. Who will remain and go from your LIFE is already fixed. God gives you the option to choose. Based on your choice the path is laid out. The ultimate destination remains fixed. Your Karma can influence your outcome and future births.

Don't bother about whether flowers will be showered or bombs shelled at you when you play. Focus on your performance and play to win.

Don't just fill your mind with positive and inspiring images. It's more important to feel those images as real.

When everyone talks and no one listens chaos prevails and resolution vanishes.

Great people are always welcomed by everyone. Those who welcome common man are great.

Try to do same thing in different ways. This would bring in innovation and may give birth to the most efficient process and systems.

Sun rises and greets everyone softly then takes a round of the whole world.

© **Life Quotes For One and All**
BY SANDEEP RAVIDUTT SHARMA

There is no substitute for excellence.

© **Life Quotes For One and All**
BY SANDEEP RAVIDUTT SHARMA

Watch the world with colourful glasses and not just by wearing black goggles. LIFE is colourful and amazing.

Find moments of joy and be happy always. Happiness comes in small small packets every day. Grab it all to make it big.

Great work lives more than it's creator.

Explore the world but don't forget to start from your own self.

If you have made criticism of others as a full time job then why don't you start with criticizing your own self.

Mother cares for you at all times even if you don't care for her. Take care of her and be ready to get Divine Blessings.

www.ingramcontent.com/pod-product-compliance
Lightning Source LLC
Chambersburg PA
CBHW031440210526
45464CB00005B/2273